The subject ma[tter] and
vocabulary hav[e been chosen]
with expert assistance, and the
brief and simple text is printed
in large, clear type.

Children's questions are
anticipated and facts presented
in a logical sequence. Where
possible, the books show
what happened in the past
and what is relevant today.

Special artwork has been
commissioned to set a standard
rarely seen in books for this
reading age and at this price.

Full-colour illustrations are on
all 48 pages to give maximum
impact and provide the
extra enrichment that is the
aim of all Ladybird Leaders.

# List of contents

A Ladybird Leader

# homes

written by James Webster

illustrated by Bernard Robinson, Martin Aitchison
and Brian Price Thomas

Publishers: Ladybird Books Ltd . Loughborough
© Ladybird Books Ltd 1975
*Printed in England*

# Home—a place to be safe in

Long ago, caves were used as homes.
A fire was lit outside.
Fires helped to keep wild animals away.

# Home—a shelter from the weather

Later, in some parts of the world,
huts were made of mud.
Each hut had only one room.
All the family lived in it.

In other parts of the world,
huts were made of stones.

Remains of these can still be seen.
Even beds and seats
were made of stone.

# Homes that can be moved

An Indian wigwam

A home in the desert

Some tribes lived
by following animal herds.

They needed homes
that could be moved.

Tents were made from cloth or skins.

A home
in Lapland

A modern tent

Even today, some people
still live in tents.
A holiday with a tent
is called camping.

9

# Roman homes

The Romans built fine homes.
Many had tiled floors
and central heating.

# How a Roman house was heated

The heat from the fire
went under the floor
and between the double walls.

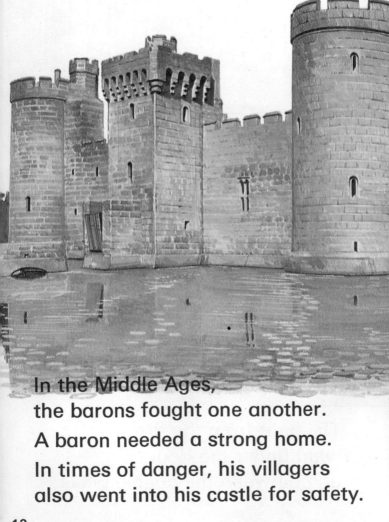

In the Middle Ages,
the barons fought one another.
A baron needed a strong home.
In times of danger, his villagers
also went into his castle for safety.

12

13

# More comfortable homes

When better laws were made,
barons no longer fought one another.
Castles were not needed.
Homes could be comfortable places.

# A home with little comfort

But many people were very poor.
They lived in homes like this,
with little or no comfort.

Today, there are many different
kinds of homes.
Some have many rooms.

Sometimes, home is only one room
which a whole family must share.

There are no other rooms
for cooking, eating or sleeping.

17

# Homes that are high up

A block of flats
is made up of many homes.

All blocks of flats need space below
where children can play safely.

# Homes that are low down

Some old houses have rooms
below ground level.

They may be dark and damp
but often people live in them.

# Homes on wheels

In North America, many years ago,
families looking for new lands
lived in covered wagons like these.

A modern home on wheels
has many of the comforts
of a house or flat.

Caravans are good holiday homes.

21

# Homes on water

These 'junks' are floating homes.
In Hong Kong, many Chinese
live on them.
They have nowhere else to live.

# Homes above water

Wooden houses once stood
on Old London Bridge.

Many were burned down
in the Great Fire of London.

A village in Borneo

The homes of this native village
are built on wooden legs.

These keep them safe and dry
if there is a flood.

# Homes can be close together

These houses are too close together.
There are no trees or gardens.
There is nowhere for children to play.
It is not safe to play in the road.

# Homes can be far apart

This is an Australian sheep farm.

The nearest house or school
is many miles away.

Children have lessons at home by radio.

# A home takes many weeks to build

Many different sorts of workers
are needed to build a house.

There must be bricklayers, plasterers,
carpenters, plumbers, electricians
and painters.

This man's job is a skilled one.
He lays the roof tiles carefully
so that the rain does not get in.

# A home can burn down in a few minutes

Houses can easily catch fire
if people are careless.

Can you think of some ways
a house can catch fire?

# An empty house is not a home

This house is empty.
No-one lives here,
so it is not a home.

# People make a house into a home

A family has moved in,
so this house is now a home.

# Two well-known homes

Buckingham Palace is the home
of the British Royal Family.

The Royal Standard is flying over it.
Do you know what this means?

The White House is the home
of the President of the United States
of America.

It is in Washington D.C.

# A 'home' above the sea

A lighthouse is a kind of home.

The keepers on duty must live there
for weeks at a time.

If the seas are rough
they may have to stay longer.

# A 'home' above Earth

A space-ship can be a kind of home
thousands of miles from Earth.

One day, some people may live
and work in space
for months at a time.

# A home made of ice

Once, when Eskimos went hunting,
they built igloos with blocks of ice.

Now, most Eskimos live
in modern homes and do not hunt.

# A modern 'igloo'

This shelter is shaped like an igloo,
but it can be put up and taken down
much more quickly.
It can be moved about very easily.

# Homes in wartime

In wartime, a town can quickly
be destroyed by guns and bombs.

Many people can be killed.

Others lose their homes.

When the fighting stops,
towns must be built again.

But it may be years
before everyone has a home again.

# The world needs more homes

Each year there are more and more people in the world.

More and more homes are needed.

Many people have to live
in huts like these.
Their homes are small, ugly
and hard to keep clean.

# Looking after a home

Homes must be painted
and kept in good condition.

To save money, some people
do the work themselves!

# Homes use up land

To grow food, good land is needed.
Grassland like this
gives cattle and sheep their food.

When homes are built,
good farmland is often used up.
More homes may mean less food.

# Homes can waste heat

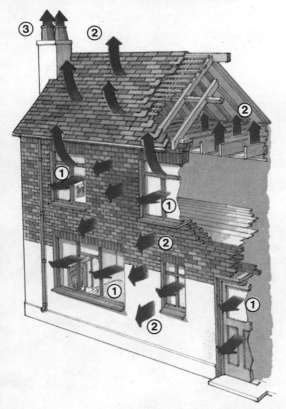

A lot of the heat in a home
is lost through:-

1. The windows
2. The roof and walls
3. The chimney of an open fire

# Homes can save heat

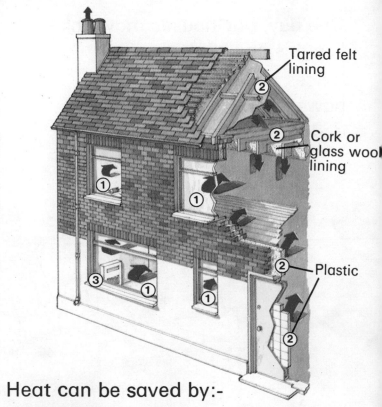

Tarred felt lining

Cork or glass wool lining

Plastic

Heat can be saved by:-

1. Two layers of glass in the windows

2. Lining the roof and walls
   in a special way (see picture)

3. A fire that sends most of the heat
   into the room, not up the chimney

# A home of the future

One day, our houses may look like this one.

It uses heat from the sun, power from the wind and collects rain-water.

1. Windmill makes electricity.
2. Water pipes in all the panels are heated by the sun.
3. Storage tank holds enough hot water to last a year.
4. Flat roof catches rain-water.
5. Tank stores rain-water from roof.
6. Windows have three layers of glass to keep in heat.

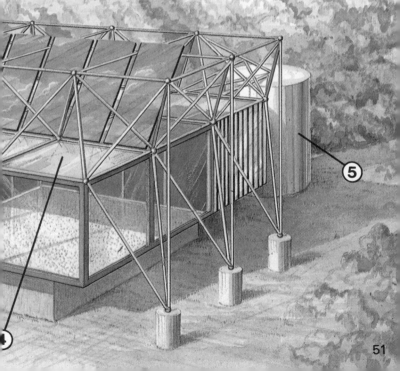

A palace

A mansion

A block of flats

A stone cottage

# ACTION ☆ FORCE
INTERNATIONAL HEROES

™

# RETURN OF THE DINOSAURS

*story adaptation by* C J Ware

Ladybird Books

Who knows where the Cobra bandits will strike next? Or what twisted scheme they are working on to dominate the world? Certainly the scientists, unearthing seventy million year old dinosaur bones far out in the desert, weren't even thinking about them.

But suddenly the silence of the desert was shattered. A lone Cobra fighter dived on their worksite.

Wild Weasel shrieked with pleasure as his lasers blasted the site on his first fire pass.

No one was hurt, but everyone dashed for cover.

Wild Weasel's jet screamed to a halt by the burning site. He climbed out and searched through the dinosaur bones.

"He must be a collector. They're desperate men!" said the chief scientist, watching from the safety of a nearby boulder. "But it's strange, a true collector would have taken the Deinonychus feet – he's just grabbed the nearest skull."

Wild Weasel climbed back into his plane, carrying the skull. The engines roared to life, blasting dust across the desert.

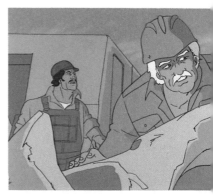

"Plan A is complete," he reported back to Cobra's secret base.

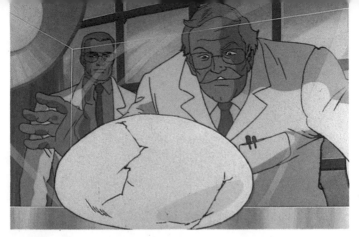

Meanwhile, at the International Science Academy, an audience of top boffins was listening to Doctor Archibald Massey. "I have cloned this egg from a single cell of the Garter Snake," he said.

As the egg hatched, the bandit twins Xamot and Tomax gave the order, from far away at Cobra HQ, for Plan B to proceed.

Suddenly an attendant ripped off his disguise to reveal his Cobra uniform.

"Hold it right there, Dr Massey," he said, grabbing the doctor.

Then the huge window behind them exploded in on the lecture theatre. A Cobra helicopter was hovering outside. From its open door, a figure aimed a huge, strange-looking weapon into the hall.

Stunned by the chaos and noise, the audience stood paralysed by fear.

Then the Cobra weapon fired loudly: not a bullet or a shell, but a huge Cobra capture net. It ballooned into the lecture theatre, and scooped up Dr Massey. Before the horrified gaze of a thousand scientists the doctor was whisked away to the waiting helicopter.

At Action Force Command Headquarters, Scarlett wanted to know, "Why is Cobra stealing dinosaur bones and old scientists?"

Action Force Warrant Officer Flint explained.

"One, Intelligence believes Cobra plans to clone dinosaurs on a base in the South Pacific. Two, Dr Massey has developed a Rapid Growth Catalyst. One plus two equals a way of growing full size dinosaurs in twenty four hours!"

Just then Deep Six radioed in from patrol in the South Pacific: "Hey, this is weird! I've found an island that's not on the map!"

"That's not so odd, Deep Six. We're on our way," said Flint.

Within seconds, the Action Force Sky Strikers were winding up to full strength, as Action Force prepared for takeoff.

But the key to opening an attack is surprise – and the strikers had now lost that key because they were seen approaching the island.

As the Action Force Planes skimmed over the jungle, the undergrowth parted to reveal some very unpleasant machinery.

Miniature radar dishes tracked the approaching Action Force aircraft, feeding information through to a computer.

Heat-seeking Cobra rockets automatically locked onto the three Sky Strikers as first Flint, then Scarlett, then Gung-Ho flew in low.

Suddenly the rockets screeched straight to their targets.

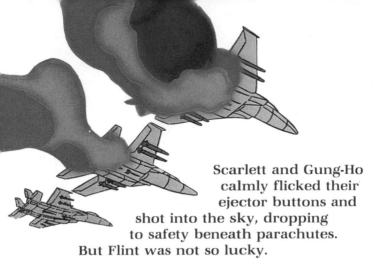

Scarlett and Gung-Ho
calmly flicked their
ejector buttons and
shot into the sky, dropping
to safety beneath parachutes.
But Flint was not so lucky.

"My controls are jammed," he shouted,
struggling to straighten the plane.

"Bale out!" screamed Scarlett. But even as
she and Gung-Ho watched, the stricken Sky
Striker went into a steep dive – and straight
into an evil-looking swamp.

Not far away Cobra Commander was giving orders to his captive, Dr Massey, who was terrified. "Each bone fragment hasss enough cellsss to clone eggs for an infinite number of living dinosaursss," he hissed. "I need all those dinosaursss. Therefore I sssuggest you begin now!"

As Cobra Commander stood over him threateningly, Dr Massey worked quickly to produce the first dinosaur eggs seen on the earth for seventy million years. Within twenty four hours the huge and terrifying monsters would be roaming the earth again.

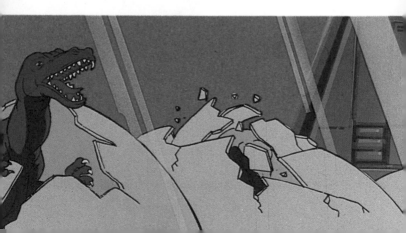

Cobra Commander looked almost affectionate as he held in his hands the first tiny dinosaur that hatched.

"You are going to grow to rule the earth onccce more, my little one," he crooned.

"Inject the growth hormone. I want thessse little beautiessss to grow!"

Meanwhile, Destro worked on the cybernetic mind control discs which were to control the fully grown dinosaurs.

He and Cobra Commander knew exactly how to turn the dinosaurs into their slaves.

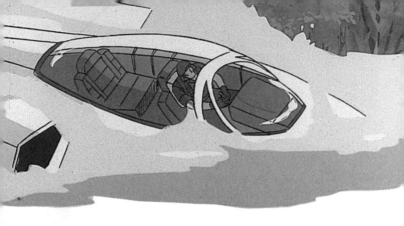

As the dinosaurs were bursting out of their shells, Flint was ploughing into the swamp.

Scarlett and Gung-Ho saw the smoking wreck of Flint's Sky Striker disappear from view.

"I thought he was going to make it," said Gung-Ho, as they turned sadly away.

Then the swamp stirred at their feet and out crawled Flint.

"I blasted the cockpit canopy with my hand laser and baled out just in time," he said casually.

"Am I glad to see you!" said Scarlett with relief. "This operation was tricky enough without cutting down the odds to two against Cobra!"

"I'm sure you would have coped. Gung-Ho has enough fight to even things up!"

"I sure got an appetite, too," moaned Gung-Ho.

Flint turned away and began hacking into the jungle.

"Er, Flint, do you know where we're going?" asked Scarlett, after two hours of hard work and listening to Gung-Ho's rumbling stomach.

"Looks like we've got to where we're going," replied Flint. His machete cut through one more clump of undergrowth: there was the Cobra fortress.

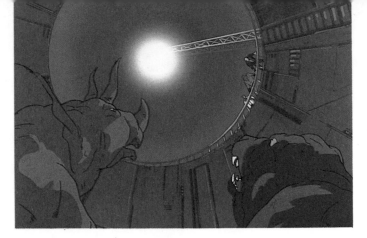

As Cobra's cameras tracked Action Force through the jungle, Cobra Commander gloated over his new, rapidly growing dinosaurs.

"Onccce I have brain beamed my little petsss, they will ressspond to my every order," he screamed, wild with delight.

"Not without the cybernetic control disc I have here!" sneered Destro.

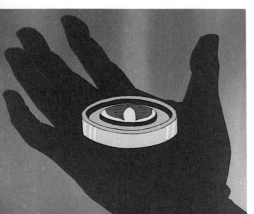

"We will try! Releassse the dinosssaursss! They will deal with Action Forccce!"

Beneath the fortress a huge steel door raised and released the creatures.

"Stop! You must feed them first!" cried
Dr Massey. "Without food they will perish."

"Feeding them isss what I had in mind," said
Cobra Commander. "Dessstro, let me try the
mind control disc. Dinosaurs, find the Action
Force Team," he ordered.

Out stamped the terrifying herd. Gung-Ho
stood his ground, but his laser lances bounced
off the dinosaurs' tough skins.

Cobra Commander and Destro happily watched on their screens as the prehistoric herd chased Action Force.

But Action Force were not so happy.

"Somebody's watching us," yelled Scarlett, pointing at a camera.

"I'll soon fix that!" said Gung-Ho, swinging his aim from a dinosaur to the camera.

It exploded with Gung-Ho's first shot, but by then the dinosaurs were almost upon them.

Now that Destro couldn't see the action on his video monitor, he couldn't give commands, and the dinosaurs lurched about out of control.

Destro ordered his Crimson Guards to reinforce the dinosaur attack.

The dinosaurs used their own brains now. They forced Action Force back into a cave, and sent in the smallest of the herd to ferret them out.

Flint, Scarlett and Gung-Ho backed off as one
of the dinosaurs leapt at them. It rolled Flint
over like a toy and sank its razor teeth deep
into the soft back of his uniform kit-bag.

"It's looking for something to eat!" shouted
Scarlett.

The pack rations kept the beast busy long enough for Flint to wriggle free.

Scarlett pulled the rations out of her own kit-bag and fired them on her cross-bow to behind the line of leering Crimson Guards outside the cave.

Instantly the dinosaurs chased after the food, trampling the Crimson Guards' vehicles.

Action Force charged out of the cave after them, Flint pausing only to grab some dynamite which was strewn among the wreckage.

Action Force now had a clear run back to the foot of the fortress.

Scarlett and Gung-Ho scaled the sheer rock, and used a small explosive charge to break into the Cobra control room.

Before they did anything else, they had to capture the cybernetic control disc which controlled the dinosaurs.

Meanwhile, Flint set about dynamiting the base of the fortress, then followed the others.

The fight was tough. Gung-Ho and Scarlett were outnumbered, and they had little chance against Cobra Commander and his crew.

Just as they were overpowered, Flint's

dynamite rocked the fortress and opened up a way into the base.

In the chaos, Scarlett managed to grab the cybernetic control disc.

"Dinosaurs, attack the fortress!" she ordered.

Crazy with hunger, the dinosaurs returned the moment Scarlett spoke, smashing walls and doors as they came in.

As the fortress crumbled about them, Destro, Tomax and Xamot realised that their plans were wrecked. Using Destro's personal propulsion arm rockets, they shot to freedom through a shattered window.

The fighting in the control room stopped when an enraged dinosaur burst in. Everyone was on the dinosaur's menu; it wasn't fussy.

"It's time we got out of here," said Flint.

"For onccce I think you're right!" agreed Cobra Commander.

Cobra Commander led the dive for freedom
– and the avalanche of bodies, including
Dr Massey – down the rock face. When Flint
recovered at the foot of the hill, he looked
round. "Where's Cobra Commander?" he asked.

"He must have slithered into a hole," said
Gung-Ho. "And it's time I slithered off and
found some food."

"Well," said Scarlett, looking
at the herd of dinosaurs now
contentedly munching
through the wreckage of the
supply dump. "You may
have to share
some with
your friends!"

"Move over
boys, I'm
famished,"
joked Gung-Ho.

"Cut out the wise-cracks," snapped Flint. "I've a feeling it won't be long until Destro, Tomax, Xamot and Cobra Commander slither out from under their hiding place.

"The dinosaurs are staying. But we are leaving. Come on, Dr Massey." And with that, they went.

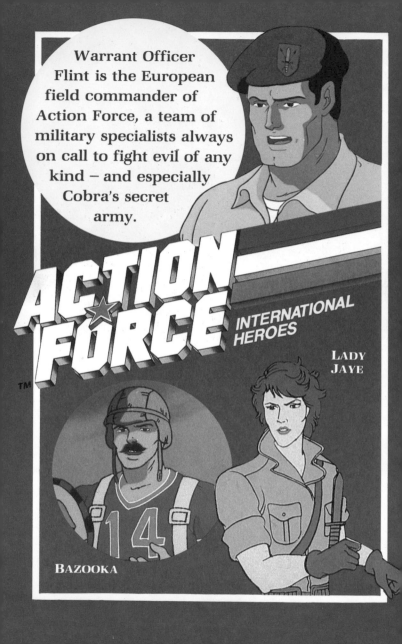